Tom Brady
SUDDEN
GLORY

TRIUMPH
BOOKS
CHICAGO

Contributors

Photography
AP/Wide World Photo
Sportpicts
Joe Robbins
John Williamson
Tom DiPace
Bruce L. Schwartzman
Tomasso DeRosa

Linc Wonham ... Editor
Ray Ramos ... Designer

This book is available in quantity at special discounts for your group or organization. For further information, contact:

Triumph Books
601 South LaSalle Street
Suite 500
Chicago, Illinois 60605
(312) 939-3330
Fax (312) 663-3557

Printed in the United States of America

ISBN 1-57243-531-3

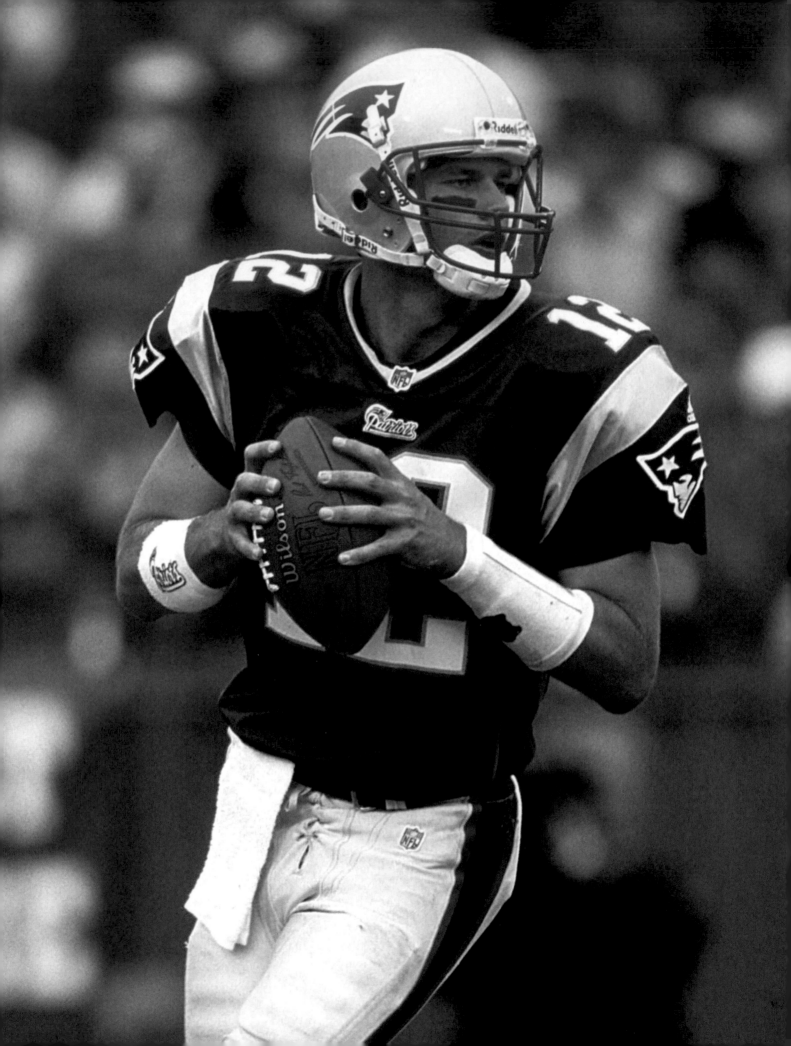

The Quarterback Challenge

It used to be an impossibly tough job, and then somewhere a few years back things took a turn for the worse. Sonny Jurgensen, who labored 18 seasons in the National Football League, once remarked that playing pro quarterback was "like holding group therapy for 50,000 people a week."

The position is among the most visible, the most demanding in all of sport. As Jurgensen or any other Hall of Famer will tell you, no other role draws a more emotional response from the fans. Over the course of a game, quarterbacks and their publics run the extremes of love and hate, admiration and spite. There is seldom a middle ground.

"Pro football gave me a good perspective to enter politics," former Buffalo Bills QB Jack Kemp once quipped. "I'd already been booed, cheered, cut, sold, traded, and hung in effigy."

It should be pointed out that Jurgy and Kemp both played in the days before mega-million-dollar contracts. The fans they faced were actually mild compared to the testiness you find in modern stadiums, where ticket prices are outrageous and beers cost five bucks.

Nor did the old timers have to contend with learning high-tech offenses, reading complex, multiple defenses, and listening to a haranguing coach over the helmet radio headset.

All of which means that playing quarterback today is more challenging than ever.

In Search of Greatness

The basic job still requires that same old tricky mix of talents. Leadership and the passing gun rate high. But so do fearlessness, competitive spirit, physical toughness, presence of mind, mobility, excellent vision, luck, determination, and a knack for winning. Add to that a level of self-confidence that routinely borders on arrogance and you have a recipe that few athletes can concoct.

Which is just the reason that the entire sport—from ballboys to general managers to season-ticket-holders—maintains a fascination for young quarterbacks. The question is always there, hanging in the

The Quarterback Challenge

air with the barked signals and the singular smell of pads and sweat: is he the one?

More often than not, the answer is a resounding no.

The corridors of the NFL's stadiums are littered with the lost hopes placed in the likes of Cliff Stoudt, Mark Malone, Browning Nagle, Timm Rosenbach, Todd Marinovich, and a host of others. The league has spent huge sums hoping that one or more of them would emerge on the path to stardom.

Throughout the early nineties, this QB star search reached new levels of intensity as the league's established old guns—Joe Montana, Randall Cunningham, Steve Young, John Elway, Dan Marino, Jim Kelly, and Warren Moon—creaked closer to retirement. On their heels followed a group of bonus-baby draft picks tabbed as the perfect candidates

to assume the mantle as the next great collection of QBs. Rick Mirer in Seattle. Heath Shuler in Washington. Ryan Leaf in San Diego. Their teams presented each with the requisite big-time contract, and then watched as they promptly slipped first into a sea of despair, then into ignominy.

"Slipping is Crash's law," Emily Dickinson once wrote. She must have been thinking of a hotshot young NFL quarterback trying to find his way in the face of overwhelming pressure to produce.

The immense fun in all of this for the fan has always been the rise of that great, unexpected dark horse. Johnny Unitas, the 19th-round pick out of Louisville who gritted his way to glory. Or Joe Montana playing his way off the trash heap at Notre Dame. Brett Favre coming out of Southern Mississippi,

Hall of Fame coach Walsh sees in Brady many of the same qualities he saw in Montana.

then finding his way onto the depth charts in the Packer organization via a stopover in Atlanta. Or Kurt Warner stocking those grocery shelves, then discovering his game and his golden arm in arena ball.

Like dozens of other prospects, each of them showed the combination of skills and luck necessary to get a shot at a starting job in the NFL. But the only way to keep it is to win. That, said the late, legendary Paul Brown, is the real test of a signal-caller: did his team win?

Many get their shot at greatness. Only the tiniest few (just 23 men have quarterbacked a Super Bowl–champion team) are able to make something of it, to win and win big.

"A True Champion"

Now we add young Tom Brady to that list. A seventh-round draft pick with hardly any pro experience, he came from the proverbial nowhere to lead the New England Patriots on a tiptoe jaunt through the regular season and playoffs and from there to a most improbable win in Super Bowl XXXVI over the favored St. Louis Rams. In a few short months, Brady had gone from little-used reserve to Super Bowl Most Valuable Player, a story that hero-hungry New Englanders gobbled up with delight.

But it wasn't just fans left blinking in surprise. Brady's performance had left dumbfounded observers with the realization that he possesses qualities that are impossible for talent scouts to read.

Among the surprised was Hall of Fame San Francisco 49ers coach Bill Walsh. "I see the same qualities in Tom that we see in Joe Montana," Walsh told the *Providence Journal*

following Brady's Super Bowl performance. "He showed complete poise and presence under the most extreme, severe pressure of the game. Plus, considering the time factor, he performed as well as or better than he normally does. He rises to the occasion, but most importantly he has the poise and presence to play his best game. That's the mark of a true champion."

It's that ultracompetitive nature that rare champions share. "I've been like this since I was about seven years old," Brady said of his drive. "I remember playing video games and wanting to win so badly. Any time I got in a competitive situation I felt that way, and I always feel like I could come out on top. It's not a fear of failure, it's joy of success. When you know what it's like to win, you don't want anything else.

"When I played baseball [he was good enough as a high school baseball player to be drafted by the Montreal Expos], I wanted to go four-for-four. If I went three-for-four, I wasn't happy about that one at bat. Competition is about not being complacent and self-satisfied. You learn to compete against yourself. Say you go to the gym and you're going to run for a half hour on the treadmill. Some people get tired after 20 minutes and leave. If I get tired by 20, I try to run for 40."

What follows is the story, in words and pictures, of Tom Brady's rise to a glory so sudden that he didn't see the fame coming—the magazine covers, the gossip-column items, the television specials, all things that increase the pressure of the job, things that will take young Brady to the next step of that very big quarterback challenge.

"Climb on My Back"

It could have been nothing but painful, this business of Tom Brady and Drew Bledsoe trading places. Surprising as it was, one's decline and the other's rise shouldn't have been unexpected. After all, if you play quarterback in the National Football League, it seems fairly obvious from the get-go that people are looking to plant a hurtin' on you.

All told, there are probably a million different ways to get whacked and sacked, and Drew Bledsoe had already discovered about 900,000 of 'em in his career as the New England Patriots' franchise player. Which makes you wonder why he decided to take on New York Jets linebacker Mo Lewis during the fourth quarter of that fateful Sunday afternoon of September 23, 2001.

Certainly it had much to do with the fact that the Patriots had lost their first game of the season and now were behind in this second game. Another season was about to turn sour for them. Bledsoe's team needed a win in the worst kind of way, and he was simply trying his best to make that happen.

He was pushing for extra yardage near the sideline. The force of the blow he took was stunning, shearing a blood vessel in Bledsoe's chest and tearing an artery near his rib cage. He would lose seven pints of blood. Twice.

"I was trying to scramble and kind of have the option to go out of bounds or come back in and get the first down," he would explain after he got out of the hospital, where doctors had finally controlled the internal bleeding. "As I tried to lean back in and get the first down, [Jets defensive lineman Shaun Ellis] grabbed my legs so I ended up being exposed. And Mo put a good hit on me. Obviously a clean hit. Not a dirty hit by any stretch of the imagination.

"When I landed, I don't believe I lost consciousness. If I did it was very, very quickly. As I got up and walked down the sidelines, my trainer and medical staff asked me what the score of the game was, where I was, and I was able to answer all of those questions correctly. So I was allowed to stay in the game.

"Then after the next series I went to [Patriots third-string quarterback] Damon Huard and I was asking him some questions about our two-minute offense and some specific plays. I think that he, from the questions I was asking, determined that I wasn't functioning in my full capacity. That was probably when the decision was made to take me out of the game."

It wouldn't be until later, when he tried to get undressed in the trainer's room, that team personnel decided they'd better get Bledsoe to a hospital in a hurry.

Down and Out

The loss of Bledsoe was another huge blow to a team that was already struggling through a strange season. First, there were management's continuing battles with wide receiver Terry Glenn, which had left Bledsoe's top target suspended and threatening lawsuits. Beyond that, there was the mysterious neck injury to linebacker Andy Katzenmoyer, the back surgery for defensive standout Willie McGinest, and a host of injuries to the offensive line.

Then, in August, 45-year-old quarterbacks coach Dick Rehbein died suddenly from a heart condition. The team was still reeling from that blow when terrorists struck the World Trade Center and the Pentagon on September 11. Patriots guard Joe Andruzzi's three brothers were New York City firefighters.

The league had suspended play in the surreal days following the attack. When the games resumed on that September 23, they brought with them a return of the Patriots' misfortunes.

The loss of Bledsoe seemed to have marked the death knell for a team that had seen its once-bright promise slip away in recent seasons. Bledsoe, after all, had been the darling of New England since his arrival as the top overall pick in the 1993 draft as a 20-year-old bonus baby out of Washington State.

"When he first came into the league, he was such a little kid," explained former Patriots offensive lineman Eugene Chung. "You'd look at him and say, 'He's a little kid.' But when you'd see him throw that ball, you'd say, 'Wow! This kid is gonna be a man, a man amongst boys.'"

Bledsoe's arm started a turnaround in the fortunes of the once-awful Patriots, who had just finished a 2–14 season before coach Bill Parcells drafted Bledsoe. Bledsoe's talent very quickly excited his veteran teammates.

"The first time I saw Drew in training camp his rookie year, I knew I'd never played with anyone like him before," said Pats tight end Ben Coates. "It's his height, and the way he throws the ball so well. His ball really gets up on you fast. He'll hit you in the face mask if you're not careful."

"Drew can throw any kind of pass," agreed former Pats quarterback Steve Grogan. "He reminds me of a young Marino."

Faced with big expectations after Bledsoe's rookie year, the Pats had slumped to a 3–6 start to open the 1994 season. But Bledsoe and New England's young defense found their maturity.

They fell behind Minnesota 20–0, then rallied to win 26–20 in overtime. Bledsoe set NFL records for passes and completions that day by going 45 of 70 for 426 yards and three TDs. "Drew kind of took over," said Pats fullback Kevin Turner, who caught the game-winner in overtime (during which Bledsoe was six for six).

It was Bledsoe's serious injury against the New York Jets that created an opportunity for Brady.

"It was a good thing for him," Parcells said, "and we needed it badly. After that, we knew we weren't out of any games. It was a tremendous confidence-builder."

The Rise and Fall

New England closed out the 1994 campaign with a seven-game winning streak to finish 10–6 and earn a wildcard playoff spot, the team's first appearance in the playoffs since 1988. Bledsoe had thrown for a league-leading 4,555 yards in just his second year in the league. The Patriots would pay dearly for that arm. Soon he was making tens of millions of dollars.

In the aftermath, replicas of Bledsoe's No. 11 jersey appeared in store windows all over New England. Long cool to the Patriots, Boston-area fans fell in love with the team—and Bledsoe. Venerable *Boston Globe* columnist Bob Ryan even declared that Bledsoe was "becoming the Patriots' answer to Teddy, Bobby, and Larry," referring to the famed Boston legends of Williams, Orr, and Bird.

Such talk brought cautionary posturing from Parcells. "Does he have the arm to be great? Yes," the coach told reporters. "But there's a lot of guys at the bus station with great arms. Great is a rare quality. We don't have enough evidence yet."

"I tell him he's going to be judged by how his team performs," Parcells had said during

Bledsoe's early tutelage. "What did his team accomplish while he was the key player? I think that's how we're all judged in athletics. I think he understands that."

At least part of the answer came in 1996, when Bledsoe, then 24, helped lead New England to the Super Bowl against the Green Bay Packers and Brett Favre. Bledsoe threw four interceptions and the Patriots lost. In the wake of the defeat, the hard-driving Parcells promptly left the team after a falling-out with owner Robert Kraft.

There was some celebration among the players after the autocratic coach departed, but things did not go well for the Patriots in the years after Parcells. His replace-

ment, Pete Carroll, proved ineffective, and Bledsoe and his huge contract were left to shoulder the pressure. Parcells had long pushed Bledsoe on his tendency to throw interceptions, a tendency that all strong-armed QBs must overcome. It would never be a problem that overwhelmed him, but it ate at his success. Over his years in Boston, he would throw 166 TDs and 138 interceptions.

Things really began to fall apart for the Patriots in the middle of the 1999 season. From that point, they would win just 7 games while losing 17 through the end of the 2000 campaign. During that time, the team would average just 16 points a game.

Bledsoe (11) and Brady (12) never let the quarterback competition get in the way of their friendship or their support for one another.

"Climb on My Back"

Throughout the downturn, it was still clearly Bledsoe's team. But the quarterback knew, as Parcells had often reminded him, that, fair or not, he would be judged on the team's wins and losses.

Then came defensive-minded Bill Belichick, who had replaced Carroll after the 1999 season. Belichick had labored in Cleveland for five unsuccessful seasons during which he acquired a reputation for lacking communication and public-relations skills. Indeed, Belichick was a wonk, far more comfortable spending hour upon hour dissecting videotape of games than he was communicating with the press—or with his own players for that matter.

All of which meant that the Patriots seemed caught in their darkest hour on that Sunday in late September 2001. Their franchise player was seriously injured, and their coach was not the kind of guy to step up and motivate them to play over their heads. Even worse, their backup quarterback was a 24-year-old California kid who had thrown just one pass in his NFL career.

An Unlikely Candidate

Tom Brady had been a sixth-round pick in the 2000 draft, the 199th player and the last quarterback selected. The NFL's talent experts had decided to take every other available quarterback ahead of him, including Chad Pennington, Giovanni Carmazzi, Chris Redman, Tee Martin, Mark Bulger, and Spurgon Wynn.

The scouts pointed out that Tom Brady, a prolific passer for the University of Michigan, had a "poor build." At 6'4", he had finished the 1999 season weighing just 195 pounds. By draft day 2000 he was up to 211, but the league's talent prognosticators considered him "skinny and narrow." Tom Brady lacked the physical strength, they said, plus he was a step slow and lacked the kind of passing arm that a quarterback needs for greatness.

It was skinny, slow, weak-armed Tom Brady who stepped up to address his veteran teammates that September Sunday after Drew Bledsoe's nasty injury.

The veteran leadership on a football team is sort of like the chorus in a Greek tragedy: they say how the show is going to go. They can sense a fraud in an instant. And they can mock and ridicule readily if they sense they're working alongside a quarterback who can't get it done. It is standard practice for veteran leadership to make life miserable for pretentious young quarterbacks. Ryan Leaf learned that lesson in San Diego the hard way.

The circumstances didn't bode well for Brady that day. Still, he offered one message for his veteran teammates: "Climb on my back."

Much later, when people worldwide marveled at what Tom Brady had accomplished, he would be asked repeatedly how he was able to do it despite the fact that he didn't seem to have the talent for it, at least not in the eyes of the scouts.

"Never believe what others say about you," Brady replied. "I know what I'm capable of. It's far greater than what a lot of people expect."

A Hero in the Making

University of Michigan coach Lloyd Carr strolled down the hallway of his office in Ann Arbor that September Sunday and noticed his assistant coaches gathered around a television set. They were intently watching Tom Brady as he tried to lead the Patriots to a comeback win over the New York Jets with a two-minute drill.

Just as he had done for Michigan so many times, Brady executed expertly. With eight seconds to go, he just missed on a deep toss to receiver David Patten. On his last-second effort, Brady had to throw into heavy coverage. The pass failed, and the Patriots lost. But Carr wasn't surprised that Brady had been immediately effective as an NFL quarterback.

"He's not just a guy who wants to throw passes," Carr would later explain. "He takes the intelligence part of the game very seriously. He's not a loud guy, but he has a tremendous intensity."

It would be just one of many attempts to sum up Tom Brady's intangibles over the course of the Patriots' improbable 2001 season. Actually, it was a process that had begun in 2000 when Belichick decided that the underrated prospect might be a player who could help his struggling club. Belichick was most interested in the fact that Brady had completed 62.3 percent of his passes at Michigan. That number said a lot, the coach figured.

But then Belichick got a closer look at Brady in training camp and saw a slow kid with a lazy drop technique. It took Brady more than five seconds to run the 40-yard dash, which left Belichick doubtful if the kid could function in New England's quick-hit passing offense.

Belichick told Brady about his doubts, told him that he needed to hit the weights. And this is where Brady passed his first big test. He spent the entire season and off-season lifting, making every team workout, plus following his own regimen. By the opening of his second season in the league, Brady had added 15 pounds of muscle and turned his soft, slow body into a hard machine ready to compete.

When he wasn't lifting, he was working on his drop-back motion, in practice and at home at night in his apartment. Then he spent more time studying himself on videotape, tinkering with what he saw, trimming fractions of seconds off the process.

When he wasn't watching himself, he studied the game's ancient masters, especially Cincinnati's Ken Anderson. "One of the best technicians," Brady explained. "He gave attention to detail on play-action, dropbacks, the release of the football, how to lead receivers."

Beyond that, he spent every minute he could soaking up the wisdom of Dick Rehbein (and would later be rocked by his death). By the time training camp opened in July 2001, Brady was built to impress.

Belichick immediately saw the difference. In fact, the coach had been disturbed by the lack of work ethic among players when he first came to the team. So he had spent the 2001 off-season acquiring free agents known more for their hard work than their talent. That kind of player makes for a stronger team, Belichick figured.

Brady obviously fit right in with that perspective. And his numbers in the Patriots' preseason games proved it. He led all of the team's quarterbacks by completing 30 of 53 passes for 375 yards and two touchdowns with no interceptions.

Suddenly Brady went from battling highly regarded Michael Bishop for the third-string job to challenging veteran free-agent Huard for the backup spot at quarterback. Belichick loved his poise in the pocket, how Brady stood in there in the face of the rush and put the ball where it needed to be.

"Climb on My Back"

"I think it went pretty well, pretty much what I expected. I feel a lot more comfortable than I did last year," Brady told reporters. "You get out there and you start to feel comfortable with everything, and when that happens your athletic ability takes over. You just start making better reads and better throws.

"I think the ball is just coming out faster, quicker. I think I'm moving a little better, but I'm still working on that every day. There are so many things to improve on. I'm so far from where I want to be that I'm just trying to make that headway."

His improvement left the hypercompetitive Brady eager to play. But he had also established a solid friendship with Bledsoe and considered him a mentor. "In a way, you don't really want to have to go in because that means somebody got hurt," he told reporter Michael Felger at the start of the season. "But I'm going to prepare every day like I am going to play—just like Damon will and just like Drew will. If that point comes, then I'm sure Damon and I will be able to step up to the challenge."

A Hard Road Ahead

The first steps were somehow both cautious and big. On paper, it seemed like a huge challenge. The 0–2 Patriots with untested Tom Brady at quarterback next faced the undefeated Indianapolis Colts and Peyton Manning.

Only problem for the Colts was that their one-two punch of Manning and running back Edgerrin James had never won in the swirling winds of Foxboro Stadium. Belichick planned to turn loose his Bryan Cox–led defense with the hopes that Brady could be quietly efficient.

In the uncertain days before the game, Cox, one of the Pats' recently acquired free agents, stepped up with the emotional leadership that had marked his career. "They ain't going to cancel the season," he said in asserting that the Pats would adjust to the setback of losing Bledsoe. Yes, Brady was young, but he projected a confidence that his teammates sensed. Wide receiver Bert Emanuel told reporters, "It's unfortunate whenever you lose your number one guy, but we have a lot of confidence in Tom that he can step in and make the plays that need to be made."

Tight end Jermaine Wiggins offered a simi-

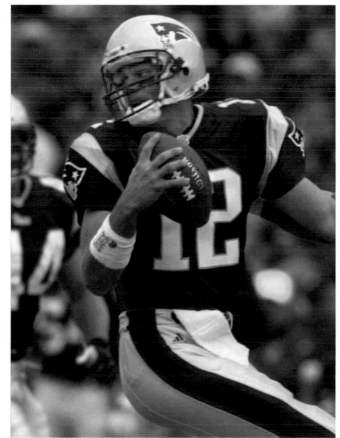

lar assessment: "When you respect a guy, you work hard for him and I think we don't have a problem with that here. The guys respect Drew and the guys respect Tom Brady and Damon Huard. I don't think you'll see a drop-off."

The main theme to emerge was that whatever Brady did, he didn't have to do it alone. And that, in fact, proved to be the case on September 30, 2001.

The defense, led by Cox, set the tone. Instead of each player being introduced individually by the pregame public-address announcer, the entire 11-man group rolled onto the field in a fist-pumping show of unity.

The display helped to ignite an emotional surge that charged the Patriots to an overwhelming 44–13 upset of the Colts, fueled by two interception returns for touchdowns, one from Amos Smith, the other from Ty Law.

"We're not a bad football team," Cox said afterward. "We suffer a little from confidence problems because of what's gone on here the past few years. But we did what I thought we could do."

Brady did his part with a mistake-free show of poise that raised eyebrows. He completed 13 of 23 passes for 168 yards and no touchdowns or interceptions.

The coaches had wisely narrowed the focus of the offense to help him adjust, and the young quarterback supplied the rest. "It just seemed like our day," Brady said. "I expected to go out there and do well. I've been preparing for this all along. It's not like they pulled me off the street and said, 'You're starting.' "

To New England fans, however, it sure seemed that way. Many of them began wondering, "Who is this guy?"

Another huge surprise was the emergence of the running game, absent for long stretches during the team's miserable run. Against the Colts it produced an incredible 177 yards, including 94 yards and two touchdowns from back Antowain Smith.

"We believe we have a good team," defensive back Lawyer Milloy told reporters afterward. "It's time to step up and start dictating the play."

"Everyone is happy," Cox agreed. "Everyone is rejuvenated. But we haven't done anything yet. We have to continue to press. We didn't win the Super Bowl today. We've got a game next week."

Indeed, they did. What awaited them was a 30–10 shellacking by the Dolphins in Miami that would have doused the life from a lesser team. The defense disappeared, the special teams suffered breakdown after breakdown, and the offense looked like the Patriots of old—unable to produce.

Brady's low point came with a fumbled snap by his own goal line in the third quarter that resulted in a one-yard touchdown return for Miami. The mistake pushed the Pats deeper into the hole, 27–10.

His passing game? Just 12 of 24 passes for 86 yards. No interceptions, but no juice either. Sitting on the sideline was veteran backup Huard, but Belichick never moved to replace his young starter.

Afterward, Brady said the total team failure had resulted from a poor week of practice. "We just have to fight our way out of this and there's nobody who is going to help us," he said. "Everyone is going to tell us how bad we are now, but we are the only ones who can affect how we play."

Afterward, Milloy spoke with Brady, who had also talked with Huard and offensive coordinator Charlie Weis.

"We're going to rally around him," Milloy said of Brady. "He's in that position. He's still a leader in my eyes."

Moving On

With a 1–3 record, the Pats had to cross the continent to play Doug Flutie and the San Diego Chargers. In practice on Monday, Belichick dug a hole and buried Sunday's game ball. Forget the bad day, he told his players. Move on.

What lay ahead was the game that laid the foundation for all that followed, both the team's and Brady's success. In San Diego, the Patriots charged from 10 points down to tie the game and force overtime, where they won, 29–26.

"You're 1–3, you're down 10 points, and your season is basically make-or-break," the young QB told reporters afterward. "What happened today just shows that the guys in here want to fight. It shows that when you're willing to put it all on the line, good things happen."

The game-winner was a 44-yard Adam Vinatieri field goal four minutes deep into

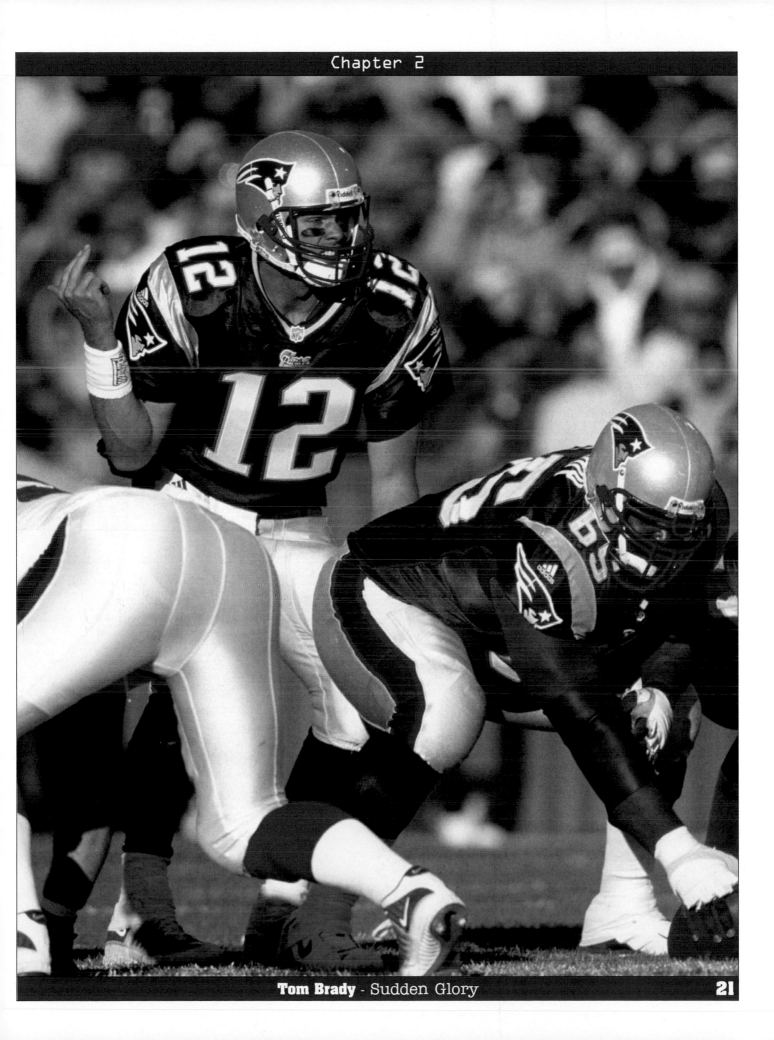

overtime. To survive, the Pats had been forced to overcome breakdowns on defense and special teams. "It showed we have some heart," Milloy said.

Especially the young QB.

Down 26–16 with 8:48 left in regulation, Brady displayed real mental strength, completing 10 of 16 passes for 101 yards in the last two drives of the fourth period. He tied the score with a three-yard throw to tight end Wiggins. The only problem was that there were 40 seconds left on the clock. Flutie and the Chargers rushed back, but their 59-yard field-goal attempt fell short.

In overtime, Brady made a veteran-like read of an interior blitz by the Chargers, and quickly called for maximum protection with a check off at the line. Then he tossed deep and exposed interference against wide receiver Patten. The whopping penalty, a 37-yard mark off, helped set up Vinatieri's winner.

"They were bringing the house," center Damien Woody said. "He checked to max-protect and got it done. I've been saying all along, he doesn't play like an inexperienced quarterback. He saw there was a situation and he put us in position to take advantage of it."

Led by linebacker Junior Seau, the Charger defense had hopped up and around the snap count for much of the day, clearly planning to rattle Brady. He answered with a varied cadence that produced just the opposite effect. Ultimately, it was the Charger defense that fell victim to three encroachment calls.

If any of his teammates still doubted Brady, all they had to do was look at the stat sheet afterward: 33 of 54 for 364 yards, two touchdowns, no interceptions.

Just as important, the game marked the return of the disgruntled Glenn, who buried his troubles with seven catches for 110 yards and a touchdown.

"It would have been a long season had we lost," said defensive lineman Bobby Hamilton. "We needed this game. It just shows you that if we continue to believe in ourselves, we can do a lot of things."

Someone pointed out that Brady was moving right along in his NFL career without ever having thrown an interception, a total of 114 attempts without a turnover. All of it was good enough to bring the national spotlight. The young QB was named NFL Player of the Week.

"The things I liked the best about his performance were his decisions with the ball—I thought he was going to the right place most of the time," Belichick said. "I thought he showed a lot of poise under pressure, stepping up into the pocket."

"It shows the type of character the guy has," Patten said. "With the game on the line like that, it just shows he's out there to make it happen."

With the win, the Pats advanced their record to 2–3, and in Monday morning's papers, Boston columnists were speculating about the need to trade Bledsoe. They pointed out that Brady was in the second year of his three-year rookie contract for $936,000, which meant that he was making only about $300,000 per season. Bledsoe's trading could clear up more salary-cap room, the prognosticators figured, showing just how quickly speculation could run wild.

The talk tempered a bit the next week when Brady's NFL record of 162 career-opening attempts without an interception came to a jarring end in a disastrous fourth quarter.

Brady's presence of mind at the line of scrimmage helped beat San Diego in overtime.

In the weird air of Denver's Mile High Stadium, with his team trailing 24–20, he threw four picks. The killer pick with just 2:24 left to play was returned 39 yards for a score, and the Pats fell back to earth, 31–20.

Brady's first pro interception came when he failed to connect with Patten in the end zone, and hit Denver's Eric Brown instead. On the ensuing series Brady overthrew Patten and Denver's Deltha O'Neal gladly hauled in the miscue.

"It's real easy when things go well," Brady told reporters afterward. "This is the hard part. This will be hard to get over, but we have to get over it."

"Every time he got to the line against us, he was looking over the defense and calling audibles," Broncos linebacker John Mobley said of Brady. "He was very much in command."

Watching from the sideline, the recovering Bledsoe told reporters that the game hadn't diminished Brady. "I believe in him totally and the team believes in him totally. He has to come back next week and play better and he will play better. This team is behind him now as much as ever."

Privately, Bledsoe advised Brady: "You're going to have more days like this. But you've got to show the team you're ready to go Wednesday."

Just as important, the defense stepped up and took the blame for the loss. "[The defense] needs to start contributing more so this young offense can develop," said safety Milloy. "We can't put them in adverse situations. We put [Brady] in that situation. When he's stress-free, he's second-to-none."

Receiver Troy Brown, who admitted dropping a couple of passes, said the fault was his, not Brady's, on at least one interception.

"He was reading for the [defensive back] to do one thing and I did another. I screwed it up," said Brown. "My expectations are that I'll make those plays."

If nothing else, the team's poor performance pushed a new set of buttons in the Boston sports talk-radio debate over the team's quarterbacking situation.

Settling In

Strangely undaunted, the Patriots recovered on the road in Indy's RCA Dome, whacking the Colts for a second time, 38–17. The defense again intimidated Indy's offensive weapons, and Brady responded with a display of steadiness, completing 16 of 20 passes to five different receivers for 202 yards and two touchdowns. The jewel was a 91-yard touchdown pass to Patten, a Patriots record.

Then came Atlanta, where Brady shook off four sacks to complete 21 of 31 for 250 yards and three touchdowns in a 24–10 win. Suddenly, Brady's team was 4–4 and eyeing the opportunity to make the playoffs.

Their eyes grew bigger with a road win in Buffalo that lifted them above .500 for the first time in many months. Despite being sacked another seven times, Brady was an efficient 15 of 21 for 107 yards and a TD and an INT. Through the stretch came the clear impression that he was growing up under fire and looking like he was born for the job.

Meanwhile, the controversy that all of Boston had been anticipating came to a turning point that second week of November when Bledsoe returned to practice, began taking snaps, and learned that Brady was to remain the starter. **Continued on page 26**

The Brady File

It was Cowboys scouting director Larry Lacewell who came up with the "Good-Looking Guy" theory. "I think to be a great quarterback, you've got to be good-looking," Lacewell explained, "and all of them are."

It seems a good bet that New England Patriots fans of the female persuasion won't argue with that one. It all started long before he posed shirtless for *Sports Illustrated*. As each Sunday passed over the fall of 2001 and the Patriots' success grew, more and more people, especially women, wanted to know more and more about young Tom Brady. You know, the guy with that cleft chin, the blue eyes, the hunk package.

The same kind of vibe traveled through the ranks of University of Michigan coeds when Brady showed up there fresh from the California beaches as a college freshman in 1995. Who's that tall kid with the nice tan, that long, surfer-dude hair, the perfect teeth, that husky, deep voice?

Well, just another of the Brady bunch. You know, the San Mateo, California, Bradys, the stone-cold bunch of jocks, beginning with father Tom Sr., a former Phillies draft pick, and mom Galynn, who plays on a nationally ranked tennis team. Then there are the family's three older girls who, when they weren't babying little Tom, were out kicking butt in their own way: Maureen was an All-American pitcher at Fresno

State, Julie an All-Pacific Coast League soccer player at St. Mary's, and Nancy a softball player at Cal-Berkeley.

Tom Jr. fit right in with that family tradition, playing soccer and baseball when he was little because his parents thought playing football wasn't a good idea for young kids. By high school, though, he had made a name for himself at San Mateo's Serra High, something that wasn't exactly easy to do, considering that it already sported famous athlete alumni in coach John Robinson, base-baller Gregg Jefferies, football Hall of Famer Lynn Swann, and future baseball Hall of Famer Barry Bonds.

"When you walk through those hallways . . . you always think about the guys who had walked those same paths," Brady said. "Bonds, obviously, Gregg Jefferies was another one I always looked up to. And there haven't been as many football players, Lynn Swann and John Robinson. The tradition of our sports there was always pretty special."

As the years went by, Tom

Jr. developed into a left-hand-ed-hitting catcher with a future in the bigs, except that he let the scouts know that he was saving his heart for football. If he had played along he could have been a high pick, but most of the major league organizations passed on him. Hoping they could turn his thinking back to the diamond, the Montreal Expos drafted him late, then offered him big money to sign.

But the former church altar boy wanted to play college football. So started his path to football glory. Little did he know that it would eventually lead him to become regular fodder for the gossip columns, with one New York magazine offering a spring 2002 tidbit about Brady dirty dancing with diva Mariah Carey at a local nightspot.

Brady shook his head and denied much of the gossip grind, but it didn't matter. He'd reached that phenom level so quickly.

His sisters, by the way, are touting him as that dream date for the girls: sensitive, commu-nicative, soul-mate material. Here are a few quick specs:

BORN . . . August 3, 1977
HEIGHT . . . 6'4"
WEIGHT . . . 220 pounds
PERSONAL . . . A lifelong 49ers fan. As a four-year-old, he sat in Candlestick Park and watched Joe Montana throw the ultimate 49er TD pass to Dwight Clark to beat Dallas in the 1981 NFC Championship game.

"I intend to be back on the field as the quarterback of this team at some point in the future," Bledsoe responded.

Reporters found the team well prepared to answer questions about a controversy. "I just go out and play," center Woody told them. "It could potentially be a dangerous situation to have, but I think it's great. When Drew was in there everyone rallied around him, and when Tom went in there everyone rallied around him. We can't go wrong. We have two guys that can win for us."

Running back Smith, who had played for the Bills, was asked if the Brady–Bledsoe situation would come to resemble the ugly Rob Johnson–Doug Flutie standoff in Buffalo a season earlier.

"Drew and Tom are friends," Smith replied. "Every time Tom comes off the field he goes to Drew for advice. They help each other. In Buffalo, the two guys didn't care for each other. They hardly ever spoke."

Would the situation leave Bledsoe staring over Brady's shoulder, waiting for a run of mistakes, reporters asked?

"I'm glad you guys look at it like that, not me," Brady replied. "You never expect to play bad. It makes no difference to me, whether a guy is there or not there. There's not enough time in the day to worry about anyone else. It's enough work trying to prepare myself."

Then he offered the perfect assessment: "That's what has made him such a great quarterback in this league for a lot of years. . . . Who doesn't want to play? You go ask the backup running back if he wants to play, and he's going to say the same thing. And if you don't want that, you're in the wrong line of work and you ought to be working in a shopping mall."

"We're in it together," Brady added. "This is about trying to get the New England Patriots to win football games. If we were sitting here at 1–8, it would be a different story. It's good that we've won these games and we're in this position. Now that Drew is back, we're a much better football team.

"If you have any division within the team—that will never be the case here because we wouldn't let that happen," continued Brady. "We respect each other too much. But the one thing I could do to disrespect him is to say, 'Here's your job back.' That would do nothing for him."

Bledsoe pointed out that, by necessity, his position was a fine line. "I'm going to do everything I can to get back on the field and at the same time I'm going to help Tom as much as I can when he's playing," he said. "Those two things aren't conflicting. It's fairly simple. If I give us the best chance to win, then I'll go back on the field. If Bill feels Tom gives us the best chance to win, then he'll stay on the field."

Brady replied that he had no problem with Bledsoe's position. "He's a competitor."

Belichick said Bledsoe was responding just as he expected. "That's what every player should do," the coach said. "That's what this game is about. I couldn't ask any player on the team to do more than that, to come in here every day, every week, and prepare like he is going to play and win. And if we get that, we will win."

"They know that they're not hurting my feelings or disrespecting me by supporting Tom when he's on the field," Bledsoe said, his exasperation obvious both with the situation and the questions. "And the same is true if I

After losing in his first look at the Bills, Brady came back to beat Buffalo later in the season to give the Pats a 9-5 record.

go back and play. They're not disrespecting Tom if they support me. It's not a case where guys have to pick between the two of us. They can support both of us, as much as you guys [in the media] would like to make it otherwise."

Back to Business

Having weathered that first media storm, the Pats turned their attention to the high-powered St. Louis Rams, who came to Foxboro for a Sunday-night game and promptly intercepted Brady twice. He completed 19 of 27 for 185 yards and a touchdown as the Pats fell 24–17.

In the aftermath, Belichick announced that Brady would be the team's QB for the rest of the season. The coach informed his quarterbacks of the decision at a regular weekly meeting. "Bledsoe was said to be rather upset with the decision," the *Boston Herald* reported.

Somehow, despite the crowd of reporters hanging around their lockers, despite their own competitive personalities, Bledsoe and Brady were able to share a laugh about the situation. And they remained friends, a huge testament to Bledsoe's leadership and character.

And Brady's loyalty. The first teammate to arrive at Massachusetts General Hospital after Bledsoe was injured? Tom Brady.

That didn't mean the situation wasn't just short of mind breaking. "Man," Brady complained. "The same questions every week."

The best salve was a 34–17 home win over the New Orleans Saints in which Brady threw for 258 yards and four touchdowns, a performance bolstered by Smith's 111 yards rushing.

"When you're able to run and play-action pass, we're pretty tough to stop.

That's our game," Brady said. "We're starting to really come into our own. It's the kind of stuff we have to build on, the kind of stuff we have to continue to do if we want to stay in the race."

"I think it's pretty clear-cut," Belichick told reporters afterward, adding that his announcement about the quarterback situation had set the tone for the performance.

The win nudged New England back over .500 at 6–5.

"Tom was hot, but it was a combination of everything," said center Woody. "Now we've got to keep it going. I'm sick of these single wins here and there. It's crunch time now. We've got to string some things together."

That string seemingly would come in a blur, a narrow 17–16 win the next week in the Meadowlands against the rival Jets, with Brady a marvelously efficient 20 for 28. With 1:46 left, it was third-and-two for the Pats. They had that one-point lead, they were at midfield, and Belichick wanted Brady to run for a first down.

"That's definitely what you want, huh?" Brady asked during a timeout.

"It's the last play of the game," Belichick replied. "You don't have time to get a cup of coffee. Can you run it or not?"

He could. With a foot to spare. They got the first down and the win, and the Pats got yet another jolt of confidence.

On the heels of that came a home win over Cleveland, with Brady throwing for another 218 yards but goosing the talk-show banter by adding another two interceptions. Another tight win at Buffalo the next week brought another interception and the third

Continued on page 31

The Wolverine

Coming out of Serra High School in San Mateo, Tom Brady had great opportunities. One of the best was an offer from the University of California. "Cal told him that he could start as a sophomore, junior, and senior," recalled his father, Tom Sr.

Young Brady, though, was more interested in Michigan, a Big Ten program with one of the greatest traditions in all of college football. Some observers pointed out that Michigan was only offering a scholarship because coaches there feared he might go to the University of Illinois.

The Wolverine coaches, however, were honest about his chances to play. "Michigan said, 'We already have six quarterbacks,'" the elder Brady recalled.

His family leaned toward Cal as the best choice, but Brady was allowed to choose for himself. He wanted the Wolverines, which meant that he would have to compete against some daunting talent, including Brian Griese, Drew Henson, and Scott Driesenbach.

"What happened was that Brian Griese and Tom were competing for the same job," coach Lloyd Carr recalled. "At the time, [Driesenbach] was the starter, Griese was the backup and Tom was third string. He started to think about transferring because Griese had two years of eligibility left and the other guy had three. I told him that he was probably being premature about it, but that he should talk to his dad and then come back to me.

"He came back the next

morning and said, 'Coach, I'm going to prove to you that I'm the best quarterback you have, and I'm going to stay here.'"

"It helped in every aspect of my life," Brady said of his decision to tough it out against the stiff competition. "When you're taught to work hard for everything that you get, you come to expect that you have to work for it. When something's given to you, it's like a gift. It's expected."

First came a battle with Griese for the starter's role, a battle that Brady lost. "That was a heck of a battle he put on," one of his coaches recalled. "I know he was bitterly disappointed."

Once Griese moved on to the NFL, Brady had to contend with the younger, but super-talented, Henson. "I've become more of a leader on the field, more of a confident player," Brady said heading into his senior season.

Somehow, he persisted and posted a 20–5 record as a starter in Ann Arbor. The highlight of his Michigan career was his last game, where the Wolverines fell behind Alabama by two touchdowns in the 2000 Orange Bowl.

Brady rallied his teammates to a 35–34 overtime win over the Crimson Tide. He did it with a 33-of-45 passing performance that included 344 yards and three touchdowns.

It wasn't his first dramatic comeback. "My favorite that season was the one at Penn State—down by 10 points, with six minutes to go," Carr recalled. "Tom had thrown an interception that went back for a touchdown, and he takes us back on two incredible drives [for touchdown passes] where any mistake by a quarterback would have ended it."

Brady finished his college career ranked second behind Elvis Grbac with the most touchdown passes by a Michigan QB in a single season, 20 in 1999. His 5,351 career passing yards are the fourth best in school history, his 35 career TD passes are the fifth most in school history, and his 2,636 passing yards in 1998 were the second most behind Jim Harbaugh's 2,729 in 1986.

"It sounds almost fake," Brady said of his hard college lessons. "But just to be a part of the Michigan tradition, to play quarterback, to be captain, the relationships I've had with the guys, the coaches who coached me—I'll never have anything negative to say about my experience.

"It's everything I could ever ask for. People say, 'God, Tommy, you had a tough time. Would you change where you went?' I'd never change a day I spent there. It's the greatest experience of my life."

straight game without a touchdown pass. But the Pats were now 9–5 and charging toward the playoffs.

Controversy-schmontroversy. Mobbed for autographs seemingly everywhere he went, Brady told one interviewer, "These are the best of times."

Fueling his success were the grueling hours he put in studying film of each opponent. He was determined not to be outworked.

"I think I have a much clearer understanding of their coverages, their blitzes, their corner play," he said before facing a Bills team that had bettered him in their first meeting. The second time around would be another battle, but he was well prepared.

The drive to push his team to the playoffs had kept Brady lifting weights, tuning his body, all the while battling the huge mental load of quarterbacking a pro team. "Mentally, it's probably a little bit tougher than physically," he said. "Physically, that's what you can prepare for. Mentally, it can get to be quite a grind. Because every week you're putting all your energy, emotion, and focus on one opponent, and then you play the game and it's out the door."

And he continued to rely on Bledsoe's tutelage, following his advice on getting proper rest and taking advantage of days off.

Now the Pats found themselves entertaining the Dolphins in a game that would decide the AFC East championship. They answered all questions with a 20-point outburst in the second quarter that propelled them to a 20–13 win and a 10–5 record.

Brady did what he needed to do, completing 11 of 19 for 108 yards, a touchdown, and no interceptions. Most of the day he spent handing off to Smith, who rushed for a career-high 156 yards.

The win put them in first place in the division, a position they secured on the last weekend of the season, blowing out the Panthers in Charlotte, 38–6. New England finished the regular season 11–5, and Tom Brady, who had started the preseason as the fourth-string QB, was named to the Pro Bowl.

Brady had completed a whopping 64 percent of his passes for 2,843 yards with 18 TDs against a dozen interceptions. Better yet, he had driven his club to an 11–3 record as a starter. But Brady's fame had grown far beyond his numbers, with his grin sporting the covers of magazines, his name in newspaper headlines, and his image driving the ratings for cable TV highlight shows.

How had all this occurred, reporters wondered? How had he survived behind the Pats' smallish offensive line? How had the running game come alive? And the defense jelled?

A big part of it had to do with Brady's onfield demeanor. Was it possible a young quarterback could take on veteran teammates when they'd made a mistake?

"He has a good feel of when to jump on a guy," Belichick revealed, "and when to explain things."

He also likes to talk a little trash, even drawing a fine for taunting opponents when he hit on a big play. "I'm pretty chirpy," Brady admitted. "I can talk a little too much smack."

Now would come the playoffs. After a first-round bye, the Pats would meet the Oakland Raiders in the second round, where the ultimate test awaited young Tom Brady.

All of New England wanted to know if he was up to the challenge.

Weathering the Storm

Brady continued to post impressive numbers and team-oriented stats throughout this most special of New England seasons. He completed over 70 percent of his passes during a four-game stretch in November, only the fifth player in NFL history to achieve that record for accuracy (the others being Sammy Baugh, Steve Young, Troy Aikman, and Brady's hero, Joe Montana, all present or sure Hall of Famers, all quarterbacks who led their teams to pro championships). Brady's 63.9 percent completion percentage for the season was the highest in team history, a further indication of his comfort zone within the team context.

When inevitable struggles did arrive in 2001, Brady only drew on further reserves. Time would prove, eerily, that he was a superior leader. Anyone who doubted that need only ask the Oakland Raiders, the Patriots' second-round foe in the divisional playoffs at Foxboro Stadium.

Expected to be the dominant team in the AFC in 2001, based largely on a 12–4 2000 season (second in the American

Football Conference), the Raiders had endured their own struggles in 2001. Though the team had added Jerry Rice, probably the best wide receiver in NFL history, there were problems in creating the prerequisite chemistry needed to win.

There had been assorted injuries on the defensive line. But probably most disconcerting, the game's best young head coach, Jon Gruden, had reportedly grown unhappy with his role in the Raiders' organization. The previous year Gruden's subtle control had virtually eliminated the Raiders' prior weaknesses—turnovers and penalties. But there was speculation in the press that he would leave the club after the 2001 season, speculation that ultimately proved correct.

Amid distractions, the Raiders' overall team discipline (something that was never much to begin with) had waned. Their outstanding placekicker, Sebastian Janikowski, had temporarily left the team to cope with personal problems.

Nevertheless the Raiders had a decided edge in experience in this game against the

Patriots. New England had been a playoff team under Bill Parcells, but that success seemed a generation ago. They now had fewer than 15 players remaining from the 1996 team that had lost to the Green Bay Packers in the Super Bowl.

More telling, Brady hadn't competed in anything even remotely close to this playoff showdown in the NFL. There was the understandable expectation that the Patriots, though they were at home, were the team that had everything to prove.

Mirror Images

As the game unfolded, the Raiders were the confident aggressors; the Patriots were seemingly in weary retreat. The traditional swashbuckling Oakland image of bravado held up, while the Patriots desperately played catch-up, identifying themselves recognizably as an underdog in need of their fans' sympathies.

Perhaps the most fascinating subtext of this game was the quarterback matchup. The Raiders' veteran quarterback, Rich Gannon, had been typecast as a serviceable backup earlier in his career, scarcely a player able to lead a team to a championship.

Yet that had all changed in 1995 with his sterling performance in relief as Elvis Grbac's replacement for Kansas City. His team lost to the Indianapolis Colts in the divisional playoffs, but the emboldened Gannon played brilliantly thereafter. He later moved on to Oakland, where arguably he was the NFL's Most Valuable Player both in 2000 and 2001.

Gannon's path to success was a clear model for Brady, the fledgling—for Gannon's perpetual fight for success and recognition was won because of his dedication to the game, his resilience,

and his willingness to spend countless hours in both the weight and the film rooms.

When Brady initiated his own rise, he remade himself physically in the weight room too, winning the respect of the players in the trenches. And like Gannon, Brady possessed huge amounts of quarterback smarts.

Bledsoe, for example, had noticed Brady's acuity in reading defenses from the beginning. "Rather than sit back and relax as a third- or fourth-string quarterback, he really was valuable in our meetings," Bledsoe explained. "He took advantage of his rookie year. He got stronger. His work ethic really allowed him to have the success he's had this year. He's honestly earned everything he's received this year."

Against the Raiders Brady would need to draw upon every reserve.

One for the Ages

The game would prove to be one of the most memorable in NFL history. It was played on a Saturday night in January in southern New England.

At this time of year, fierce weather should always be anticipated. On that night, prognostications were for clouds to roll up during the afternoon, and for a hard storm to descend that night.

This proved true. Snow fell heavily throughout the night and in archetypal fashion, the Raiders and the Patriots contended not only with each other, but also with nature.

"I looked downfield during the final drive," Patriot guard Joe Andruzzi would explain afterward, "and I didn't see yard markers. I saw a series of drifts and small hills."

Earlier in the season, Belichick had the team watch a documentary about voyagers conquering the trials of a brutal journey in the Antarctic. Now the mission had turned decidedly real. The night before the game, the coach had turned to something less metaphorical: he showed the team tapes of its game in the snow against Buffalo, from the previous season.

The conditions in Buffalo had forced the team to cope. There, Bledsoe repeatedly utilized his tight ends. This combination of character traits and football tactics would become even more important against Oakland.

Drawing on momentum provided by a maddening crowd at Foxboro Stadium, Brady immediately took the Patriots downfield, the key being a play in which he connected with back J. R. Redmond on a 19-yard pass. But conditions immediately dictated strategy. Belichick passed up a 38-yard field-goal attempt, and the Patriots' effort on fourth-and-two failed.

Almost immediately thereafter, the game seemed to belong to the Raiders.

Throughout a scoreless first quarter, Oakland moved the ball relentlessly as Gannon and Raider back Charley Garner quickly identified themselves as the players best able to adapt to the conditions.

The Patriots' season appeared over until officials reversed their ruling on an apparent Brady fumble in the fourth quarter.

"The weather was the same for both teams," Gruden noted then. "We handled it. We were forced to handle it."

Gannon seemed to put together a perfect combination. In the first half, he completed 10 of 14 passes. Though the running game faltered, Gannon found Tim Brown and Garner for short, safe completions and seemed ready to take advantage of any given opportunity.

Finally, taking over at midfield after a Patriots miscue, Gannon engineered an eight-play, 50-yard scoring drive, capping it off with his 13-yard touchdown pass to James Jett. With the wind sending its waves of silent, black cold through the night, Oakland's first strike took on added importance.

From the press box at the old Foxboro Stadium, the *Boston Globe*'s beat writer, Nick Cafardo, looked on and couldn't help but think that the Patriots' season was in peril. He had marveled at Brady's ability to implement an NFL game plan—the best, he thought, perhaps of anyone in the league, already, this early in the player's career.

Yet Cafardo couldn't help but wonder: were the nerves creeping in? After the initial drive, Brady had appeared overmatched. Offensive coordinator Weis had opted for a mostly conservative strategy in the first half. But now Oakland had the lead, and with its renowned ability to close in for the kill, the game seemed to belong to the Raiders.

Cafardo remembered thinking of how Brady had initially responded to crisis during the season. He had taken his team to a glimpse of victory against his former Michigan teammate, Brian Griese, in Denver. But then the walls had crumbled; suffering the ignominy of a four-interception fourth quarter, Brady and the team fell 31–20.

But Brady had bounced back instantly. Right after the game he eyed interviewers directly and warned the writers that his defeat that afternoon was but momentary, that he would come back.

And he did. The following Sunday he was brilliant, completing 21 of 31 for 250 yards and three touchdowns. There would be other small crises, indeed, including the game in Buffalo when an onrushing Bill had knocked him cold. But he had come back then, too, despite dizziness, to provide a win.

Yet despite the kid's past success, Cafardo remained skeptical that night.

New Life

In the locker room at halftime Belichick met with Weis and Brady and decided to open the offense up. Obviously, the young player couldn't disband caution altogether. Yet Bledsoe had included assertive moves offensively in the windy drifts against Buffalo, moves that Brady had seen on tape.

Now he had to do likewise and move the team more forcefully—because he knew what Oakland's intent would be in the decisive third quarter. The Raiders' approach would be to close out this game. This was how veterans like Brown, Rice, and Charles Woodson excelled. They had earned their honors because they understood winning's complexities.

The weather worsened, the snowflakes steadily forming a continuous sight line. The teams adapted, but the tempo of the game remained in Oakland's favor.

Vinatieri managed a field goal but Oakland's Janikowski answered with two of

Patriots coach Bill Belichick watches the action against Oakland in the two teams' memorable AFC Divisional matchup.

his own, the second a marvelous 45-yard parabola through the night. Oakland now had a 13–3 advantage.

The clock became the big pressure for Brady. He seemed to push the next drive off to a big start with a 13-yard completion to Patten, but things quickly unraveled, and New England gave up the ball with only 12:29 remaining in the game.

The Patriots' season now finally seemed to have been exhausted. Conditions, if possible, seemed even more precarious, with players unable to maintain footing as ice formed.

Somehow, as Gruden pointed out later, Brady delivered. "This game was about making plays," the Oakland coach said. "And Brady found a way."

"Our defense was so resilient all night," Brady explained afterward. "Antowain Smith had been great for us on the ground. But we were running out of time. I turned more to Jermaine Wiggins."

Brady had remembered the openings the tight ends had created in that Buffalo game film, and throughout the remainder of the night Wiggins highlighted an improbable Patriots comeback. Brady utilized Wiggins as his key receiver, mixing quick looks to him with passes to Patten and the irrepressible Brown.

Brady stepped back in the pocket and threw the cold football low, with zip, the ball creating its own strange sound in the dead of winter. As the crowd awakened late, the Patriots drove 67 yards in 10 plays to cut the lead to 13–10 with 7:52 left.

Certainly the defining moment of Brady's young career had come on this drive. It was second-and-six on the 6-yard line with the season on the line.

Brady had utilized the no-huddle offense throughout the second half, and on this play he read the defense, sensed the pressure, and bolted up the middle for the touchdown. He highlighted the play, naturally, by diving into the end zone and rolling around in the snow, for just a moment.

The game now became a race, nerves against time. It came down to a critical stop for the Patriots. Oakland's Garner charged, and defensive tackle Richard Seymour of New England repulsed the charge.

Finally, out of timeouts, New England halted Oakland again near midfield, and the Raiders chose not to try a crucial fourth-down conversion. It became a critical moment, especially after Troy Brown returned Shane Leckler's punt 27 yards to give New England a final legitimate chance. This would set up yet a final twist in the drama.

The Call

Brady had been moving the team because of his confidence in the pocket. Oakland defensive coordinator Chuck Bresnahan sensed the time was right to strike, and he went for broke.

The Raiders' Woodson flew in from the right flank, untouched, and as Brady retreated to pass, Woodson made the perfect tackle, jarring the ball loose as Brady's arm either did or did not go forward. Initially, the ball was ruled a fumble, and Oakland recovered. On the sidelines, the Raider bench erupted with limitless joy, players in white rushing out to embrace one another.

Only moments later, the signal came down from the replay officials: referee Walt Coleman would review the call. After endless reviewing of the play, the referee reversed the call. Coleman said, "It was obvious that his arm was coming forward. He was trying to tuck the ball and they just knocked it out of his hand. That makes it an incomplete pass."

Later, the imperturbable Brady said, "Yeah, I was throwing it. But I had to control my emotions. We still needed to take advantage of the opportunity."

New England followed his lead. In the second half, when he completed 26 of 39, he finished the job. On the following play after the contro-versial, unforgettable reversal, he found Patten for 13 yards to put the ball in field-goal position.

Despite having no timeouts and therefore no time to have the field cleared of snow, Vinatieri converted the 46-yard field goal, the ball driving through the snow, eerily inner-directed, tying it at 13–13 at the end of regulation.

In overtime Brady coolly led his team to victory in the arctic conditions, starting from his own 34. The play-by-play tells it best:

Brady out of the shotgun to Redmond for one yard. Brady to Redmond for 20 yards to the Oakland 45. Brady to Wiggins for two yards. Brady to Redmond for three yards. Brady to Wiggins for six yards. Brady to Wiggins at the Oakland 30 for four yards. Redmond up the middle for a one-yard loss. Brady to Brown for three yards. Brady to Patten at the Oakland 22 for six yards. Smith up the middle for four yards. Smith again for one yard. Smith once more for eight yards to the Oakland 9. Smith for another two. Then Brady over left guard to the Oakland 5 for two more.

From there, Vinatieri punched the final shot through the snow, a 23-yarder.

"We needed a two-minute drive to win the game," Brady explained. "We've gone into overtime, played in bad weather, played at night, and we've been in a lot of bad situations. And it's made us strong. At no point in time did anyone ever give up."

Least of all Tom Brady. Now he would be quarterbacking his Patriots in the AFC Championship Game. Who knew just how far this brassy young guy might take them?

Chapter 4

A Twist of Fate

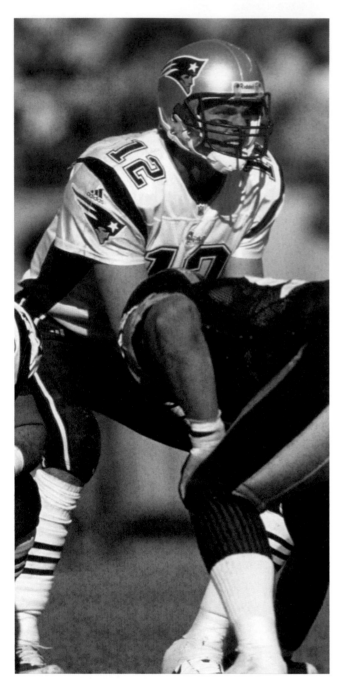

The feel-good Tom Brady story didn't end in the American Football Conference Championship game, as many had predicted it would. But it did take a hiatus.

And for one last brief time, Drew Bledsoe reinserted himself into the picture. And that seemed just fine with everybody, including Brady.

Bledsoe hadn't played a down since his blood-gushing injury on September 23. But the AFC title game in Pittsburgh proved an appropriate time for a comeback.

The Steelers had been favored (odds makers listed New England as 9 1/2-point underdogs), but the Patriots played conservatively in the first half—as Belichick loved to do—which was good enough for a 7–3 lead and the ball with a couple of minutes left in the second quarter.

It was there that Brady's left ankle twisted under him when he was hit by Pittsburgh safety Lee Flowers. He limped off to the locker room, and with 1:40 left on the clock, Bledsoe took over.

"I've done this for a long time and at times at a pretty high level," Bledsoe, who had signed a 10-year, $103 million deal before the season, later told reporters. "I felt confident coming out. I've been working hard and preparing for this exact scenario."

"You don't give a guy $100 million if you don't think he can be a championship quarterback," Pittsburgh's Flowers quipped later, when reporters asked how the Steelers felt about seeing Bledsoe. "He's a good quarterback. Nobody on our sideline was celebrating when Brady went out."

Duty Calls

Bledsoe lined up and went to work, taking the Patriots 40 yards in four plays.

A Twist of Fate

He completed all three of his passes on the drive, the last of which was an 11-yard scoring toss to Patten that put New England up 14–3 at intermission.

Just as important, he didn't hesitate on his one rushing effort. In fact, he gained four yards on the ground.

At halftime, it wasn't clear how badly Brady was injured. He stood on the sideline and watched as Bledsoe got the call for the second half.

It was Patriots receiver Brown who had caused much of the damage in the first half with a 55-yard punt return for a touchdown. The Steelers opened the second half with purpose, driving from their own 32 to the New England 16, where the Steelers attempted a field goal.

The Patriots' Brandon Mitchell blocked the kick, and Brown picked it up from there and zipped a lateral to teammate Antwan Harris, who rolled 49 yards for the TD that put New England up 21–3.

"Antwan started calling my name and I looked over my shoulder and gave it to him," Brown said.

It seemed like just enough to finally quiet the normally raucous Pittsburgh fans and their Terrible Towels. Linebackers Willie McGinest and Ted Johnson had led the Patriots defense in shutting down Pittsburgh's running game.

But just when things looked impossible for the Steelers, quarterback Kordell Stewart led them back. He completed 24 of 42 for 255 yards on the day, and helped push his team to 10 quick points. Suddenly, the New England lead was four.

Bowl Bound

New England's answer was to turn to Bledsoe, who would post just the kind of numbers that Belichick loved out of his quarterbacks: 10 of 21 for 102 yards, one TD and no interceptions.

Bledsoe did just enough to get his team into position for Vinatieri's 44-yard field goal that made it 24–17 three minutes into the fourth quarter. In the end, the defense forced two late interceptions out of Stewart, and the Patriots were going back to the Super Bowl.

No one was happier for Bledsoe than Brady.

"It feels great," Bledsoe told reporters in the midst of the championship celebration. "It's been a great year for our team but a difficult year for me personally. To have this happen . . . it's just a little bit overwhelming."

"Call us Cinderella. Call us destiny's team," Brown crowed. "We came out and proved we are the best team today."

Lining up as their next challenge would be the St. Louis Rams, who would open Super Bowl week as 15 1/2-point favorites.

Before they got to the game itself, though, there was more uncertain terrain for the Pats to cross. Reporters immediately wanted to know Brady's status, and Belichick's thoughts on the quarterback situation.

"You need a couple of quarterbacks in this league," the coach said. "I'm glad we had them today."

Jubilant in the locker room with his teammates, Brady said he felt fine but didn't know yet if he could play the next week. Asked about any quarterback controversy, Brady replied, "I'm feeling good, and that's all Coach wants us to say about it."

A Super Ending

A coach always reserves the right to change his mind. If anybody is aware of that, lord knows it's Belichick.

After all, he was the guy who accepted the head job with the New York Jets in 1999 and kept it all of one day, arriving on the Meadowlands scene for an instant, then bolting to take the position in New England, leaving then Jets executive Bill Parcells dumbfounded.

Then there was the matter of Bledsoe's early season injury. Belichick had assured Bledsoe that when he returned, he would have the right to challenge Brady for his old job.

Thinking he would step back in where he left off, Bledsoe rushed to get healthy only to find that Belichick had decided he liked things just as they were. And it was a good thing he did, because it certainly worked out well for the Patriots.

But now, as his team headed into that great media firestorm known as Super Bowl week, Belichick hesitated strangely. Maybe he figured it wasn't so good to keep saying one thing, and then doing another.

Whatever the reason, Belichick walked

into the first big media availability session that Monday in New Orleans knowing that the one and only huge question he would face would be the one about his quarterbacks.

Who would it be in Super Bowl XXXVI? Bledsoe or Brady?

The throng of assembled reporters asked that question 50 different ways. And Belichick seemingly found 50 different means of replying that he wasn't sure, that he wouldn't be sure until Wednesday.

"I'm not in a position to do it right now," Belichick said.

Reporters wanted to know the severity of Brady's injury, which hadn't seemed all that severe (they pointed out that he got off the plane in New Orleans looking like the very picture of health).

"I don't know. We're not even 24 hours after the [AFC Championship] game. It's too early, really," the coach said.

Suppose Brady's healthy, will he be the automatic starter?

"I will make the decision Wednesday," Belichick replied, then telling the crowd in the interview room, "You can ask the questions 50 different ways. I'll announce it on Wednesday."

Then, as a bonus, he really confused them by saying that Brady could have played in the second half of the AFC Championship game. The implication settled with a thud: Belichick had picked Bledsoe over Brady to get his team to the Super Bowl.

Mind Games

Most perplexed was Rams coach Mike Martz, who one second said he'd begin preparing to face Bledsoe, then thought better of it and said he'd prepare for Brady.

"That's something we'll address tomorrow," Martz finally said.

Belichick had managed to confuse everybody, particularly the opposition, which may have been his intent from the very start. "I'm sure a lot of people want more information than I'm able to give you right now," the Pats coach offered as an aside.

The only parties seemingly unflustered by all of this were the Patriots themselves, which is exactly how Belichick wanted it.

"It shouldn't matter who's out there," Brown said. "We've still got to go out and win a game."

"It's not going to make a difference," agreed Law. "It's not going to be a distraction to our team because we're pulling for both of them."

"We don't have any other choice than to be confident in whoever he picks," Brown added.

The Patriots themselves were much more interested in the point spread. "Underdog? We'll take it if that's the way we're labeled," linebacker Tedy Bruschi said. "But sometimes underdogs win it all."

Acting Massachusetts Governor Jane Swift had echoed those very sentiments that morning in a sendoff for the team in Boston. "While some may already believe that the Rams are a favorite on Sunday, being the underdog has suited the Patriots just fine this year," she told a crowd of hundreds that gathered in front of the state house. "The Rams are going to find out very soon that these underdogs have a very painful bite."

Kraft, Belichick, Bledsoe, Brady, Brown, and several other teammates had listened to the governor's speech before heading to the Big Easy. As promised, Belichick revealed on Wednesday what he had known all along: Tom Brady would be the starter for Super Bowl XXXVI.

It made perfect sense. Odds were that Brady wasn't going to make any early mistakes that would doom his team. And if Belichick needed Bledsoe? Well, the $100 million man would be right there on the sideline with him. He had already shown in the AFC Championship Game that he could jump right into the fray and keep things cool.

Then Belichick went out and did what he does best. He cooked up a defense that found a way to fend off Rams quarterback Kurt Warner and running back Marshall Faulk for three quarters.

More important, the defense produced two key turnovers, an interception, and a fumble, which gave Brady and the offense something to work with. It was good enough for a 14–3 New England lead at the half, a tremendous confidence booster.

Only problem was, a defense can hold an offense like the Rams' for only so long. In the fourth quarter, Warner and his teammates got it going, which meant that between them, the two teams produced perhaps the sweetest, most competitive—some would say greatest—finish in Super Bowl history.

Fantastic Finish

The Rams and Warner wore down the Patriots' defense with two long touchdown drives that tied it at 17–17. With about 90 seconds left, New England got the ball back on its own 17. There were plenty of thoughts about having Brady run down the clock for overtime, but none of them belonged to Brady himself.

"The thought of taking a knee never crossed my mind," Brady said. "I was going to go out and win the game."

Milloy (with Super Bowl trophy) and Brady were among the Patriots who took part in a celebration at Fenway Park during a 2002 Red Sox game.

A Super Ending

Belichick and his staff had been conservative all day, but now offensive coordinator Weis figured it was time to try simple, short passes.

"I walked down the bench to talk with Charlie Weis to find out what he wanted to do," Brady remembered later. "He had just finished talking with Bill. He turned to me and said, 'We're going for it.' I said, 'Great.' But he cautioned me about making bad decisions or turning the ball over. That could be the game for them.

"Drew and Damon were standing there," Brady said of the sideline conference. "They asked me what I thought would work. I gave them two or three plays. They liked what I thought. There was no timeout after the Rams' touchdown, so there wasn't a lot of time before we got the ball back. I looked at Drew just before I ran on the field, and he said, 'Throw the ball. Go for it. Just get out there and sling it.' And that's the way I thought when I went into the huddle for that final drive.

"I wasn't nervous. In fact, I don't think I was nervous once all year. The Thursday night before the Super Bowl game, I was in bed thinking, 'Hey, how come I'm not nervous? This is the Super Bowl.' I never felt nervous. The night before the game, I had a great sleep. And after the first play of that [winning drive], I felt confident we were going to do it."

Brady threw two quick completions and moved his team to the 30. With the completions came a little surge of confidence.

"When we came out and hit the first pass on them, I could see them backing off," Brady explained. "It was visible. You could see it in their faces and the way they reacted. I was confident of what we were going to see from them, and how we were going to react to it.

"The Rams had played basically the same defense in passing situations throughout the entire game. They played like Tampa Bay: two-deep zone with the safeties deep and outside. Then they drop the middle linebacker straight down the field so it's almost like a three-deep zone. It's tough to hit the deep ball on them. That's the one they are trying to take away. They make you stay patient."

Staying patient had never been a problem for Belichick's teams, and wasn't a problem for Brady either. The Patriots' offense systematically nibbled its way up the field.

But with 29 seconds left, Brady and his teammates faced a second-and-10 at their own 41. "We didn't need any touchdown, though," Brady said. "Just a 25-yard pass play and we were in position to have Adam [Vinatieri] kick the field goal."

Brady wanted to get the ball to Brown. "It's 64 Max All In," Brady said in describing the play he called. "Max means the blockers give me more time. The receivers all run in-routes. The Ram secondary reads your eyes. I looked right all the way and Troy was able to slide in underneath them to the left."

Great at catching and running, Brown took the pass and motored to the St. Louis 36. Brady wasn't done, though. He hit Wiggins for another six yards. Then he stepped up, watched the clock slide down to seven seconds and spiked the ball.

In 83 seconds, he'd nailed five of seven pass attempts, the spike counting for an eighth attempt. It would go down as one of football's greatest two-minute drills.

Best of all, it set up Vinatieri's 48-yard field goal, which shot straight through the

Brady's performance in the closing minutes against the Rams helped him earn Super Bowl MVP honors.

uprights, giving New England the 20–17 victory and setting loose an explosion of jubilation back in Boston.

"That's what's important," Brady said. "To play your best when it's all on the line."

The Rams' Warner had thrown for 365 yards, but it was Tom Brady who completed 16 of 27 passes for 145 yards and claimed Super Bowl MVP honors.

Hail the Hero

Reporters pointed out that he had been quietly consistent for three quarters while his team played a conservative game, then unleashed his arm with the outcome on the line.

"That's our team," Brady said. "It's the way we react to the pressure. Everybody steps up."

Hall of Fame coach Bill Walsh watched the final drive and told reporters: "There were about five or six key plays that [Brady] performed with total poise and presence regardless of the stakes. That separates him from just about every other quarterback."

"I'm not sure I've ever seen any player improve as much as he has," Belichick said.

As is typical of Super Bowl heroes, Brady was feted and honored over the coming months, sent to Disneyland, scheduled for all the big TV shows, photographed for all the magazine covers, interviewed for all the newscasts. "So much has changed," he would say later.

In the spring, the Patriots would announce they had traded Bledsoe to the Buffalo Bills, one of their keen AFC rivals.

"We gave up a great player," Brady told reporters. "When I was a kid and heard the name of the New England Patriots, I thought about Drew Bledsoe. It was Drew Bledsoe's

team. I felt the same way when I got drafted. Drew Bledsoe was the Patriots. Now he's gone. In one way, there's relief. This will do away with all of the talk week to week that had become a distraction for everyone. At the same time, Buffalo has a great quarterback and we have to play against him a couple of times a year.

"We had a good relationship. He helped me a lot. He is a good friend. It was a difficult situation for both of us. When I was playing last year, I knew I had his support."

The first big phase of his quarterback challenge was over. But Tom Brady had already turned to the road ahead.

"The main point is to continue to focus on the task at hand," he said as a new season unfolded, "and that's to win football games. So the emotional ride, as far as I'm concerned, it's been straight up."

In June, he came to the Patriots' minicamp obviously ready to go again. "I've been studying what I did last year," he said. "The coaches have broken down the film. You see what you did well and what you didn't do well. Then you try to find out why what happened happened. Right now, I'm in the greatest condition of my life. I came into workouts [March 1] and was even stronger than I was at the end of last season. I really didn't take any time off. When I went home after the Pro Bowl, I started lifting right away.

"I'd rather be in here lifting weights than be downtown, believe me. I look forward to coming in here and working. I love to practice. Fun for me is running seven-on-seven drills in the heat of training camp. That's fun. I love it."